GODDESSES OF INDIA

Radha Krishna's Divine Energy

SHUBHA VILAS

Om KIDZ
An imprint of Om Books International

When Earth was full of evil, and wicked men ruled the world, Krishna decided to descend from heaven and set things right. He asked Radha to take birth before him and wait for him on Earth. Radha could not live without him even for a day. So she said, "I will not open my eyes on Earth till you stand in front of me." Krishna agreed readily.

Soon after, Vrishabhanu, the village head, saw a baby girl floating on a golden lotus in the holy Yamuna. He was not sure whether the lotus was golden or it was reflecting the radiance from the effulgent infant. The more he looked at the unusual infant, the more mesmerised he felt. *Surely,* he thought, *the baby is divine.* No human could be so attractive and glowing like a star.

Filled with love, he brought the lovely child home to his wife.

When Vrishabhanu handed the child to his wife Kirti, she too felt the same magical pull. Being childless, they accepted her as God's gift to them. They adopted her and loved her more than they could ever imagine. But their joy was short-lived. Slowly, they discovered that their precious daughter was blind!

She was also deaf! And speech challenged too! She would simply not open her eyes. Nor would she respond to their words. And talking was out of the question. She was in a bubble, in her own world. And she had no desire to step out of it.

One day, Narad Muni happened to come visiting. He was actually searching for Radha. He knew she had already appeared on Earth and was impatient for a darshan of the Supreme Goddess.

When he heard that Vrishabhanu and Kirti had a daughter, he rushed there. As soon as his glance fell on the tiny bundle in the cradle, his eyes widened. He fell flat on the ground paying his humble respects to her. She was indeed the divine energy of Krishna.

Narad Muni was ecstatic but he found Vrishabhanu very sad and quiet. The parents shared with him that their daughter refused to open her eyes. She refused to hear and she also did not make any sounds. Narad Muni already knew the answer to the mysterious happening. There was no problem that Narad Muni could not solve. He suggested, "Invite Nanda Baba, Mother Yashoda, Balarama and Krishna from Gokula. They can help you for sure."

Invitations were immediately sent to Gokula. Soon, Nanda Baba arrived with his family to meet his dear friend, Vrishabhanu.

While the adults were talking, Krishna crawled all over the house. He soon reached the cradle and tried to stand up and peep inside. His tiny feet wobbled as he balanced himself to look at the lovely girl sleeping inside. Immediately, a broad smile crept on his face.

As soon as he uttered some sounds which sounded like 'Radha', the child blinked her eyes. She had been waiting for Krishna to come. She opened her eyes with the arrival of Krishna. The first words she heard were from Krishna. And the first sound she made was his name.

Vrishabhanu was overjoyed to see Radha and Krishna talking to each other in baby language. She had opened her eyes! She could hear Krishna's garbled words and she was also reciprocating with him. What a fantastic sight that was. Absolutely unbelievable!

Then onwards, Radha and Krishna spent all their time together. When Krishna played his flute, Radha and the gopis dropped everything and joined him in Raaslila.

Krishna got great pleasure in teasing the gopis and Radha. He and his friends would steal their butter pots or even break them. Once Radha got angry with him. To please Radha, Krishna dressed himself as a peacock and danced in front of her. The peacocks in the forest were delighted and started dancing with him. Unable to stop herself, Radha too joined in the dance, forgetting her anger.

She could never be annoyed with Krishna for too long.

Radha and Krishna are inseparable. Krishna, the Supreme God and Radha, his Supreme Energy. Radha is the source of all Shakti tattva. The Supreme Goddess of fortune is an emanation of Radha. All feminine energy in this world ultimately originates from Radha who is known as the internal energy of Krishna.

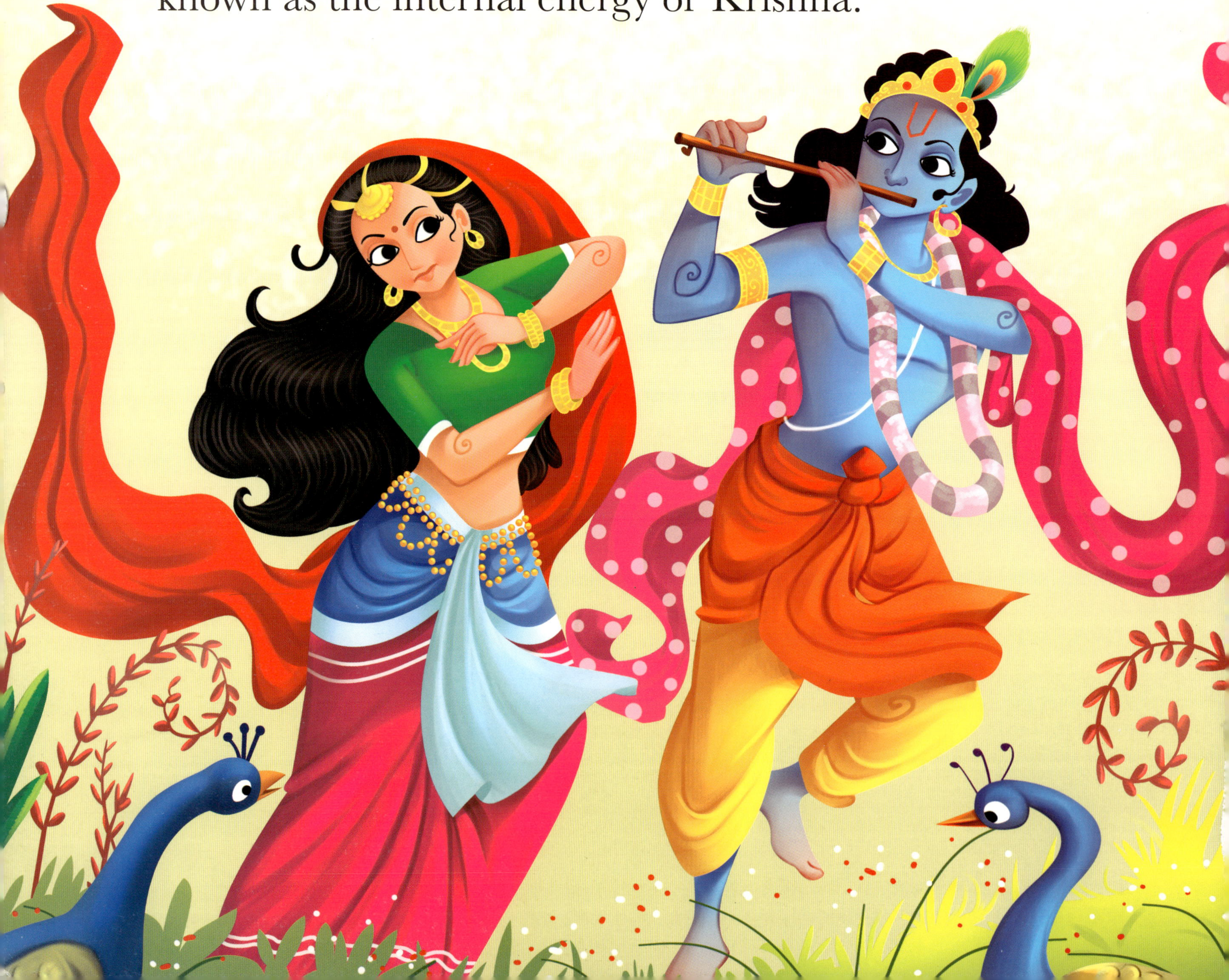